KETTLEBELL TRAINING

An Introductory Guide to Getting the Most From Your Kettlebells

(The Ultimate Kettlebell Workout and Diet)

Michael Brown

Published by Tomas Edwards

© **Michael Brown**

All Rights Reserved

Kettlebell Training: An Introductory Guide to Getting the Most From Your Kettlebells (The Ultimate Kettlebell Workout and Diet)

ISBN 978-1-990268-66-3

All rights reserved. No part of this guide may be reproduced in any form without permission in writing from the publisher except in the case of brief quotations embodied in critical articles or reviews.

Legal & Disclaimer

The information contained in this book is not designed to replace or take the place of any form of medicine or professional medical advice. The information in this book has been provided for educational and entertainment purposes only.

The information contained in this book has been compiled from sources deemed reliable, and it is accurate to the best of the Author's knowledge; however, the Author cannot guarantee its accuracy and validity and cannot be held liable for any errors or omissions. Changes are periodically made to this book. You must consult your doctor or get professional medical advice before using any of the suggested remedies, techniques, or information in this book.

Upon using the information contained in this book, you agree to hold harmless the Author from and against any damages, costs, and expenses, including any legal fees potentially resulting from the application of any of the information provided by this guide. This disclaimer applies to any damages or injury caused by the use and application, whether directly or indirectly, of any advice or information presented, whether for breach of contract, tort, negligence, personal injury, criminal intent, or under any other cause of action.

You agree to accept all risks of using the information presented inside this book. You need to consult a professional medical practitioner in order to ensure you are both able and healthy enough to participate in this program.

Table of Contents

INTRODUCTION 1

CHAPTER 1: WHAT ARE KETTLEBELLS? 5

CHAPTER 2: KETTLEBELL TRAINING 12

CHAPTER 3: CHEST AND CORE 15

CHAPTER 4: KETTLEBELLS EXERCISE 25

CHAPTER 5: BURNING FAT VS. BUILDING MUSCLE 32

CHAPTER 6: COMMON KETTLEBELL MISTAKES 35

CHAPTER 7: EXERCISES 41

CHAPTER 8: KETTLEBELL EXERCISES 50

CHAPTER 9: A FEW OTHER ESSENTIALS 59

CHAPTER 10: MAKING YOUR METABOLISM WORK FOR YOU 84

CHAPTER 11: COOLING DOWN 87

CHAPTER 12: TRAINING HACKS 103

CONCLUSION 108

Introduction

Kettlebells have been around since the early 1700s when Russian strong men wielded kettlebells of various sizes and shapes. It's interesting to note when looking at early photos of these strong men that their physiques were far more proportional and athletic then what we have come to associate with bodybuilding. Although body building started in the 1940s it really took off in the 1980s with the wide spread use of machines to enable gym owners to get more people through their doors with less training and supervision being required. Machines restrict you to one plane of movement. This relieves your stabilising muscles of having to do any of the work when using a machine and opens you up to injury when trying to control a weight in a plane of movement you have not strengthened.

This has unfortunately lead to strength training neglecting functionality in favour of mirror muscles i.e. chest and biceps. Isolation was the new term in training, which worked fine to grow the particular muscle being 'isolated' but doesn't help the body work functionally as a whole. In the last 5 years we have seen a resurgence of functional training such as Crossfit with Olympic lifts, tyre flips, kettlebells, and body weight exercises.

There is a lot to be said for minimalism in your training, as to do any more than is required is simply wasteful. With kettlebell's compound movements, you can engage multiple muscle groups at once, thereby increasing the calorie burn, improving your body's ability to work as a unit and achieving more in less time. Most of the exercise sessions only consist of two or three exercises and can be completed in less than thirty minutes. Best of all, the rhythm involved in using kettlebells makes them fun and addictive.

Using kettlebells simplifies your workouts and gym routine as you don't have to think about which piece of gym equipment exercises which muscle group along with what size or weight you need to use to achieve a workout. You don't have to figure out which days you should do cardio and which days you should do strength because kettlebells combine cardio and strength training. Many kettlebell exercises target the posterior chain, which is hugely beneficial, not only for athletic performance but also for good posture and back support. Lower back pain is often attributed to underdeveloped glutes, which in turn cause the erector spinal muscles to overcompensate, as well as tight hip flexors (caused by sitting in office chairs all day), which create back pain by causing the pelvis to tilt forward. Kettlebell training strengthens the gluteal muscles, helping to relieve the erector spinal muscles and promotes hip flexor flexibility, which reduces pelvic tilt and decreases lower back pain.

Certain kettlebell exercises build your power-endurance, which is your ability to sustain fast muscular contractions over an extended period of time; examples of these exercises are snatchs, and explosively performed squats or swings. While both strength-endurance and power-endurance are essential qualities to possess, power-endurance is usually what determines the winner in sports competitions. Power-endurance training is also an excellent approach for fat loss and conditioning.

What follows is the 80/20 rule (20% which will give 80% of the results) of kettlebell exercises and tips to get the desired results in the most efficient and minimalistic way.

Chapter 1: What Are Kettlebells?

Kettlebells are a kind of free weights, shaped like a ball with a handle to provide easy grip. There is a handle at one end of the iron-cast ball, which results in an uneven distribution of weight. The unbalanced distribution of weight results in a more extensive work out of the muscles in order to stabilize and maintain balance and counteract the momentum.

Kettlebells generally come in standardized weight of 35 pounds, but can range from 5 pounds to over 100 pounds. Kettlebells are small and portable; therefore, they can be incorporated in all types of fitness and athletic trainings.

Material of the Kettlebells

Kettlebells are usually made up of cast-iron but some kettlebells are coated with other materials like vinyl or rubber. The cast-iron kettlebell is also called the 'original' kettlebell and is most frequently used. The vinyl-coated kettlebell is essentially similar to the original kettlebell but it contains a coating of vinyl over the ball and handle of the kettlebell, which gives it a more sophisticated look. Rubber-coated kettlebells are not prone to rust or get scratches.

Cast-iron kettlebells come in black color only. Vinyl-coated kettlebells can be made in any color. The performance of cast-iron kettlebell and vinyl-coated kettlebell does not differ a lot. Vinyl-coated kettlebells may grab the skin uncomfortably in certain exercise positions.

Types of Kettlebells

There are two variations available in kettlebells, the original kettlebells and the competition kettlebells.

Original Kettlebells

Original kettlebells consist of a ball and a rounded handle made up of cast-iron. The diameter of the ball may vary based on the weight of the ball and the manufacturer. This type of kettlebell is used by people who are interested in general fitness training.

Competition Kettlebells

Competition kettlebells or Pro Grade Kettlebells are used by individuals who are kettlebell fanatics or are involved in kettlebell sport. They are more durable as compared to cast-iron kettlebells because they are made of high-grade steel. These kettlebells come with a square-shaped handle. The diameter of the ball remains constant regardless of the weight of the kettlebell. This means that whether you are using a 16 pound kettlebell or an 8 pound kettlebell, it will rest on the exact same place on your forearm. Competition kettlebells have a thinner handle to provide a lasting grip and to minimize fatigue with strenuous repetition sets.

The History of Kettlebells

Ancient History of Kettlebells

The history of kettlebells is somewhat unclear but there is archeological evidence that Kettlebells were used for strength building in ancient Greece. A kettlebell weighing 143 kg is stored in the Archaeological Museum of Olympia, Athens, Greece.

Russian Origin of Kettlebells

The word kettlebell appeared first time in 1704 in a Russian dictionary. At that time, 'Girya' or Kettlebell was only used in measuring weight of grains and other goods. The use of kettlebells in physical training had not started until the late eighteenth century.

The founder of heavy athletics, Dr. Vladislav Kraevsky, travelled through the Europe from 1870 to 1880 in order to gather information about physical sports and finding new ways to improve physical health. He introduced the Russian athletes to exercises that involved dumbbells and kettlebells.

The origin of weightlifting in Russia dates back to 1885 when Dr. Kraevsky founded a weight training hall with the goal of muscle development of Russian athletes.

The kettlebells continued to flourish in Russia but their spread to other parts of the world was restricted by the World War I and the Russian civil war.

The Russian government aimed to minimize country's health care expenses by making kettlebell training mandatory for the public. The Russian armed forces also started using Kettlebells sports as a measure of soldiers' physical strength. By 1974, kettlebell sport had been officially declared as the ethnic sport of Russia.

Kettlebells' Journey to the West

Kettlebells were not introduced in the West until the late twentieth century when a Russian physical training instructor wrote an article on Kettlebells in a popular American athletes' magazine. Inspired with the benefits of kettlebells, the Dragon Door Publications decided to start manufacturing Kettlebells in America. They approached the Russian instructor and requested him to teach American people how to use the kettlebells.

In 2002, kettlebells' popularity took off when it made it into the Rolling Stone Magazine as 'the hot weight of the year'.

Girevoy Sport

Kettlebell lifting or kettlebell sport, which is called Girevoy sport in Russian language, has a long history in Russia. In 1948, the first kettlebell competition was held in which 55 athletes took part. The athletes, who were called Gireviks, competed in kettlebell sports in three disciplines with no time limits; the press, the snatch, and the jerk.

The kettlebell sports modern history started in 1962 when rules were unified and time limits were enforced. Kettlebell lifting further gained popularity in 1985 when the first championship of the Soviet Union was organized and winner was given the title of 'Master of Sports'.

The first European championship took place in 1992, which was organized by the European Union of Weightball Lifting. In 1993, a world championship was held in which 96 athletes from 5 different countries participated. Women were allowed to take part in Kettlebell lifting in 1999.

Chapter 2: Kettlebell Training

Kettlebell training is an exercise training program that became popular recently. It has fascinated people who go to the gym and others who purchased the equipment and use them at home. They are able to swing an immensely heavy weight around. Apparently, it can be beneficial to average users as well as experienced sports personalities.

It may not actually serve as sole substitute for either strength training or cardio exercises, but it makes use of the elements in these exercises. The forceful, usually ballistic actions involved include the whole body and specific fitness areas like coordination, balance, and strength. These aspects do not get worked up, as they should be using the long-established training techniques. People have found the kettlebell training far from boring and it helps to enliven and revitalize workout routines.

Uses of kettlebell training

For a sports person, this is beneficial in building power and muscle strength. This training can help beginners who go to the gym or those who simply exercise at home to make their existing workout programs less monotonous.

Some applications of kettlebell training are as follows:

Supplementary program to your current exercise program - Some people add basic kettlebell workouts before or after their cardio exercise or strength training to add variety in the workout.

It can be a part of your exercise program. - Kettlebell exercises may be incorporated into an exercise routine. For instance, the shoulders may have additional work up by doing "clean push and press," a total body exercise that involves lifting weights. Others perform a swing prior to doing major squat exercises.

Part of a cross-training exercise program - Doing kettlebell workout can serve as a dynamic breather from your usual exercise regimen. Basic exercises like swings, presses, pulls, deadlifts, rows, and squats included in kettlebell training can provide an entire body workout. The training can also exercise the body in a manner that is different from the other routines.

Sole workout - Kettlebell training is not designed as an alternative workout for strength training or cardio exercises. However, if you are getting bored with your usual program, a kettlebell workout can be an interesting addition to motivate you into working out on a regular basis. It should be noted that it is imperative to have workout experiences prior to engaging in kettlebell training.

Chapter 3: Chest And Core

The chest and core are very important when it comes to fitness, as the muscles they possess are vital in so many everyday functions that we carry out. The chest muscles are responsible for helping to transmit power to the arms and shoulders, while the core is vital as it basically holds the upper and lower half of your body together. Having a weak core can affect everything from your breathing to your ability to do simple things like get up off a chair.

This chapter hopes to address the different ways you can improve core strength and strengthen the muscles in your chest to ensure that you not only look good, but can live the healthiest life that you can.

1. The Kettlebell Russian Twist

Target muscle group: Core (Abdominal muscles and Obliques)

Walkthrough: One of the easiest and most efficient core strength exercises there is, is the Russian twist. It is a traditional girevoy exercise that helps build up both the Abdominal and Oblique muscles in the core. This is one of the best exercises there is to build up core strength and stability, and has been proven to do more good to your core than sit ups and crunches can.

Sit with your legs bent at a comfortable angle, (less than 90 degrees) and make sure that your feet are flat on the floor, about shoulder length apart. Lean back at a 45 degree angle (taking your feet off the floor), and twist from left to right while swinging the kettlebell across your body from one side to the other. Swinging from left to right and back again constitutes one rep. The recommended number of reps per set is good but this is another one of those fluid style exercises that you can do a time trial, just to see how long you can survive the pressure.

Please take note, as well, that this is a more advanced version of this exercise. To take some of the strain off, try leaving your feet off the ground as you do the workout, and don't lean too far back.

2. The Kettlebell Floor Press

Target muscle group: **Chest, core**

Walkthrough: This crossfit exercise is very similar to a standard dumbbell floor press, but is fundamentally different in many ways. The way the weight being used behaves is by far the most significant one, as your body reacts slightly differently with the change in centre of gravity of the weight being used. The kettlebell floor press is ideal for those looking to build up strength and muscle in their chests, though it also helps with arm and core strength to a certain extent.

As with a standard dumbbell floor press, this exercise begins with you lying on your back with a kettlebell beside you. Grab the kettlebell by the handle with your palm facing inwards, and press the weight straight upwards while rotating the palm. If done correctly, at the peak of the press, your palm should now be facing your feet. Bring the kettlebell back down to the starting position to complete one rep. After the desired amount of reps, change hands and repeat the exercise to complete one set.

This exercise can be done with two kettlebell weights simultaneously, depending on the desired workout or fitness levels. With two kettlebell weights however, it is important to take even greater control of the weights, as there can be a tendency to favor one hand over the other with this exercise.

3. Single Arm Kettlebell Snatch

Target muscle group: **Chest**

Walkthrough: The traditional bar snatch has been around for as long as weightlifting has been around, if not longer. This brilliant drill is one of the prefect ways to display the explosive strength of your chest and arms, though the main provider of power is most definitely your chest. Like the traditional bar snatch, the main aim of the Single Arm Kettlebell Snatch exercise is to get your arms and the weight above your head in what looks like one fluid movement.

When doing the kettlebell snatch, remember that the posture is almost the same as with a regular bar snatch. You should be standing with your feet about shoulder length apart, with your knees slightly bent and with the kettlebell weight in between your legs. Burst up on to your toes; and while doing so, pull the kettlebell up until it reaches your chest. From this position, swing the weight above your head, then bring it back down to the original starting position. Count this as one rep. Remember to keep your elbow locked in close to your body as you lift the weight up as you can seriously injure yourself if you don't.

4. The Kettlebell Press-up with row

Target muscle group: **Chest, Core**

Walkthrough: Man has been doing press-ups for a long time. They are a fundamental part of human movement, and the movement involved is the foundation of how man gets up from the prone position with stomach laid flat on the ground. There have been very many variations over the centuries, all of them invented to make the press-ups more challenging, or to help exercise a different muscle group. The one thing that all press-ups have in common is that regardless of how they are done, your chest and your core get a workout as you do them.

The one difference between the kettlebell press-up and classic press-ups is the handle on the kettlebell. The narrower purchase on which to put your palm makes this exercise harder to execute on the weights. With the added twist of the row, this promises to be a truly different drill.

First, grab your kettlebells by their handles and get into the standard press-up position. Execute a standard press-up but at the end of the press-up, lift an elbow by squeezing the shoulder blades together and get the weight off the ground at least six inches. Lower the arm and repeat, this time using the other arm to lift the weight. Aim for a set to lie between five and seven rows per arm.

5. Single Arm Kettlebell Split Jerk

Target muscle group: **Chest**

Walkthrough: This maneuver is one of the more advanced girevoy moves there is, and is used by many to train for an explosive burst of muscle strength from the chest and shoulders. It has helped many of today's bodybuilders train for the traditional barbell jerk, as it allows for more precise control of the weights and therefore a more effective workout.

This is one of those exercises that comes after a beginning transition move, so to begin, clean the kettlebell to your shoulder, keeping it in the rack position. Bend your knees and press the kettlebell over your head, while jumping into the split jerk position. While still holding the weight over your head, slowly bring your legs back together so that you end up back in the standing position. Return the weight to the rack position to complete one rep.

As with some of the other one handed kettlebell exercises, this one can also be done with two hands to add a higher difficulty rating to it. The extra weight and use of both hands also makes balancing tricky, adding to the core strength that you stand to gain by doing this routine. It is recommended however that the Double Handed Kettlebell Split Jerk only be tried once the Single Handed version has been perfected to avoid unnecessary strains or injuries.

Chapter 4: Kettlebells Exercise

Kettlebells versatility makes them ideal for vigorous exercises that involve major muscles and in the process burning fat and building power. With kettlebells, one no longer needs to spend hours in the gym as an excellent kettlebell workout takes only 15 minutes three times a week to get the same results as with a dumbbell. This makes them an ideal training program for both men and women looking for the best results in the shortest time possible.

Kettlebells gain in popularity can also be attributed to the fact that it focuses around three core lifts- the swing, the snatch, the clean and the jerk. All these concentrate the muscle to work as a group. In the process, every single muscle is worked hard strengthening your core and building core stability. The entire body is worked in less time compared to other forms of exercise.

Benefits Of Using Kettlebells

Building lean muscle

The dynamic of kettlebell training provides the opportunity for building lean muscle, and condition the cardiovascular system. Most people forget the importance of building lean muscle when trying to get in shape. The lean muscle does not just make the body look nice but also play a key role in metabolism and energy levels helping the body burn fat.

Versatile resistance training

The versatility provided by kettlebells beats about all other kinds of training options out there. They are not only more convenient than weights and machines which use more time in terms of trips to the gym. The design of the kettlebell is in such a way that they use more muscle groups to keep the weight controlled. They work the muscles from all angles encouraging well strength building and increasing flexibility. Weightlifters, professional athletes, law enforcement officers all use kettlebells to get the resistance that helps them build strength and agility required in their profession.

Cardiovascular training

Thorough cardiovascular training is vital in all kinds of training. It helps the cardiovascular system to effectively and efficiently distribute blood and oxygen to all body parts especially the muscles and brain. The body is, therefore able to use its strength and increase the brain's ability to focus more and for longer periods. The dynamic of kettlebell routine can be done in conjunction with strength training making it more efficient within a short time.

Building self-confidence

One of the most important benefits of kettlebell training is building self-confidence in the individual. It gives more confidence to feel stronger, more flexible, be more agile and feel fit. The physical benefits of working out improve self-esteem giving the trainee more emotional energy.

Convenience

The most attractive attribute of the kettlebell is the convenience in which they allow one to train. There are very few workout programs that allow one to work out all muscles of the body in conjunction with cardiovascular training without necessarily having to go to the gym. The good thing is that the training only takes about 20 minutes three times a week. Training with kettlebells requires only a few sets of kettlebells and a training program fit for your body type and aspirations.

Portable

Unlike barbells and other training exercise equipment kettlebells are portable hence no need to miss a workout. One can even carry a couple of kettlebells when out of town or on holiday.

Full body workout

Kettlebells provide full body workout, the swigs, squats, snatches, lunges, deadlifts, and presses are all compound exercises that work on all muscle groups. This makes little exercise very effective saving time and energy.

Breaks monotony

If you have been training using machines and dumbbells and hit a plateau where you are no longer able to gain size or progress to heavier weights then switching to the kettlebell based regime will shock the system into new growth not to mention its fun. This breaks the monotony of the gym and also acts as a change of scenery.

Cheap

To get into great shape one only needs at least a pair or two of kettlebells to build functional fitness. Kettlebells are generally cheap going for about 2-3 dollars per kilogram. The money spent on kettlebells is money well spent as you will not find such value for money as in gym membership or overpriced prices for other excise equipment.

Improve coordination

When you are swinging and passing the kettlebell around, your brain and muscles must coordinate effectively in order to perform the necessary movements. This increases your hand and eye coordination and the increased coordination will transfer to all the other associated activities.

Correct imbalances

If you are used to training using machines and barbells you will find that you have a stronger side that will compensate for the weaker side when necessary. Kettlebells swiftly identify and corrects the imbalances through dingle limb exercises.

Time saving

Many individuals dismiss working out due to time constraints as they are busy with other stuff but a set of portable kettlebells eliminates this excuse as it only requires about 15-20 minutes for an intense workout plan. Majority of kettlebell workouts are short and intense. If you find yourself taking substantially longer, then it maybe time to increase your intensity and reduce your rest period.

Developing massive power

Olympic lifts such as the clean & jerk and snatch when performed, increases explosive power and places a new spin on these exercises as compared to performing them with a barbell or dumbbell.

Improves flexibility

Kettlebell exercises work on postural muscles in such a manner that they increase flexibility hence better posture for the trainee.

Chapter 5: Burning Fat Vs. Building Muscle

It is undeniable that kettlebells are a great tool for burning fat. In fact the American Council on exercise has found that the average kettlebell workout (15 minutes) burns around 300 calories. As you can probably tell, incorporating this into a daily routine can have dramatic results on fat loss and general body recomposition.

But what about building muscle and strength?

Well, as with any resistance training, it all depends on the amount of weight used and the amount of repetitions. This said, kettlebells could be used to build muscle just as much as traditional resistance training. However, due to the unstable nature of the kettlebell and it's uneven distribution of weight, it increases the stress placed on the stabilizer muscles and as a result dramatic improvements can be made in ways that traditional evenly distributed resistance training. This has the added benefit of working the core muscles and can help you achieve the abs you've always dreamed of.

Later on in this book, we will see a full kettlebell workout that incorporates, strength building exercises (low reps with heavy weights) Muscle building exercises (medium reps with medium weights) and fat burning exercises (high rep with lighter weights).

Compound movements

In this chapter you will learn a variety of different exercises you can do with kettlebells. This will show the huge variety of muscles you can target with a kettlebell based workout plan.

When performing kettlebell movements, always ensure that you have ample space and are not going to hit anybody around you. Some of these exercises are fast and have a wide range of motion so the more space the better. Always wear proper footwear when performing kettlebell movements to prevent injury and wear loose fitting clothing to ensure you are not restricted in your movement.

When learning how to perform these exercises, start practicing at a very slow speed with a very lightweight. This should teach you the mechanism for the movement and what it will look and feel like. When you are feeling confident with the movement, you can increase the speed and the weight.

Chapter 6: Common Kettlebell Mistakes

So far, we have already discussed how the kettlebell training is effective in building strength and power. It is also clear that there is a wide range of kettlebell training tools available in the market, each playing a significant role. For instance, the kettlebell swing plays an important role in boosting the body's endurance while also strengthening the posterior chain.

However, one thing that you have to bear in mind is that with kettlebell training exercises, it is not always fun and games. If you are a beginner, it is critical that you pay attention to what you are doing and how you are doing it to minimize the occurrence of injuries.

If you are just starting out, ensure that you get the guidance that you need from an expert fitness coach to help you learn how to use the kettlebell equipment the right way. Here are some of the common mistakes that you should look out for when using the kettlebell;

Mistake 1: Opting For A Heavier Weight

For beginners, it is very easy for one to get caught up with so much excitement and the temptation to push yourself too hard. Yes, the challenge is good, but you have to do it gradually so that the body is not in shock.

In other words, rather than jumping all in to start off with heavier weights, it is important that you start with what you can handle and progress slowly. When you add more weight than you can handle, you will only restrict in an improper form and increase the risk of having an injury.

Whenever you are training, always ensure that your safety comes first. The best way to do this is ensuring that you select the right weight of kettlebell. Consult with a professional when you decide to choose the weights to start training with. Ensure that you are not mixing up the measurements and weights by learning the difference between meters and centimeters; and pounds and kilograms.

Mistake 2: Generating Force By Using The Upper Part Of The Body

As mentioned earlier, the kettlebell exercises often utilize movements of the whole body. This is what makes the training sessions twice effective. Unfortunately, there are so many people at the beginner level who try hard to muscle up their way through these workouts. It is important that you realize how this might place unnecessary strain on your upper body and try not to do it.

Mistake 3: Swinging The Kettlebell Too Fast

One important thing that you have to understand is that when you swing the kettlebell too fast, you risk losing control and pulling your muscles, something that could result in serious injuries. While it is often fun to swing the kettlebell with so much force after a very long day, there is a chance that this might do more harm than good when your form is compromised.

Mistake 4: Focusing On Quantity

As a beginner, there is a high chance that you will be tempted to go overboard and push yourself too hard. If your trainer recommends that you start with ten reps, going higher than that might not be a good idea.

Trust me, finishing 20 reps with a bad form is even worse than never picking up a kettlebell simply because you are employing the wrong kind of technique. It is essential that you perform each kettlebell exercise as it is required so that you avoid the adverse effects that might cause injury. Adhere to guidelines before you can even attempt to perform any exercise at all.

Mistake 5: Putting On The Wrong Running Shoes

Like I mentioned earlier, the good thing is that you do not have to wear a special kind of shoe to do this exercise. However, this does not mean that you can wear shoes that place you at risk of injury. While it is so tempting to wear shoes with very thick soles, you have to understand that this might hinder your movements while working out.

When performing the kettlebell exercises, it is advisable that you wear shoes that allow you to naturally move your ankles, lower leg ligaments, and foot. Thick running shoes do not only cushion the heels but also tends to raise the foot off the ground causing your grip on the floor to be destabilized.

Chapter 7: Exercises

Here are just a few of the best kettlebell exercises that I recommend you learn then sue in your workouts. In my personal experience these exercises have been the most beneficial to me and my fitness success when working out with kettlebells.

NOTE: All of these exercises will be in the resource section at the end of this book, with a link to Youtube videos so you know exactly what each of these exercises look like.

Kettlebell Goblet Squat – If you have ever done a front squat then you will know how to perform these. But essentially in this exercise you begin by grabbing your kettlebell by the handle on the sides. Then with your feet shoulder width apart you perform a squat. Make sure your back is straight and you are bending your knees so that your thighs are at least parallel to the floor. Ideally you want to go down a little further than that to make these the most effective.

Kettlebell Deadlift – For deadlifts you actually have a few option because there are a couple of variations that you can perform. (See "Kettlebell Deadlft" in the resource section to see the video on how to do all of them.) The first option is to perform deadlifts with the kettlebell in between your feet. If you perform this variation you will have to perform the exercise with your feet slightly longer than shoulder length.

The second option you have is to use two kettlebells. This obviously involves you to use two kettlebells that are the same weight. You can perform this with the kettlebells in between your legs like the first variation or you can perform it with the kettlebells on the outside of your legs. Just you perform the latter, just make sure to space your feet a little shorter than shoulder length to avoid hitting your feet with your kettlebells. (Ouch!)

The deadlift is really easy. Essentially you pick up the weight and bend down at the waist. Just make sure to keep your back straight.

Kettlebell Swing – Probably the most known kettlebell exercise. This is where you space your feet about shoulder width with your knees slightly bent. Then pick up the kettlebell by slightly bending at your waist, and then swing it between your legs. Then in a fast motion swing the kettlebell up, so that your arms are parallel to the ground. Repeat. Breathing is practically important for this exercise. If you aren't breathing correctly, you will tire out really quickly.

Just like deadlifts, you can also perform the swing with 2 hands or 1.

Turkish get up – This one is a little complicated to explain in writing, so I suggest you take a look at the Youtube video in the resource section to get a better understanding how to perform this exercise correctly. But with this exercise you start by laying on your side on the floor with your legs bent. Then grab your kettlebell and lay on your back with your arm straight up in the air holding the kettlebell. At the same time you also want to bring the heal of your feet so that it your knee is straight up in the air. (Same side as the arm that you are holding the kettlebell.)

Now you want to sit up, put your other hand on the floor, and lifting the rest of your body off of the ground all in the same motion. This is all done with the kettlebell up in the air with your arm straight. Then continue to stand up all while keeping your back straight.

I know that description is confusing, that's why I strongly suggest you take a look at the Youtube video. I did my best.

Kettlebell Press – The press, or the shoulder press, is really simple. Chances are if you have been working out for a while now you have probably done a shoulder press with wither dumbbells or a barbell. But all you do is stand up stand hold the kettlebell and raise it straight up in the air above your head. Really simple to do, but also really effective for working out your shoulders.

Kettlebell Clean – This is another easy kettlebell exercise. Start with the kettlebell on the ground in between your knees. Grab the kettlebell by the handle with your thumb pointing towards you. Then in an explosive motion, lift your arm, stand up straight, and make a corkscrew motion with your arm. What I mean by corkscrew is basically lift the ketlebell over your arm by bending your elbow and have it rest on your shoulder. Take a look at the video if you get confused.

Kettlebell Snatch – Another popular kettlebell exercise. This is really similar to the kettlebell swing, but the difference is you are going bring the kettlebell all the way above your head. This one may take some practice to get used to it because you need the right amount of grip in order to make sure the "bell" part of the weight is pointing down the top of this exercise. You may also want to start this exercise by performing a kettlebell swing and then working out way up to a snatch. This will give you a little more momentum to get the kettlebell all the way up above your head. You can also use both of your hands or just one.

Kettlebell Windmill – To perform this exercise start with the kettlebell raised above you with your arm straight up in the air. Then lock your legs so they are straight and start to bend at the waist, bending at your side, while still holding the kettlebell straight up in the air. Then gently stand back up again. Repeat. Take your time with this exercise because it will take some balancing skills that you may not be used to if you have never done this exercise before.

Kettlebell Armbar – This exercise is great for increasing your strength, but it also one of the best kettlebell exercises you can do in order to help fix any shoulder pain that you have. To perform this exercise start by laying on your back on the ground. Then grab your kettlebell with your palm up. Then press the kettlebell straight up in the air above you. Now bring in the same side foot as the arm you are holding the kettlebell so that your foot is flat on the ground. Now you want to say on your side, still keeping your arm straight up in the air so that it is perpendicular to the ground. Next bring the hip and leg over, so that your lower body is facing the ground, but the arm that's holding the kettlebell is still straight up in the air. Usually you hold that position for a couple of seconds. Then bring the exercise back to its starting position.

Kettlebell Halo – This is another great exercise to warm up your shoulders to avoid injury. Start by standing up straight. Grab the kettlebell handles by the sides and begin by rotation it behind you head. Picture a halo, if that makes it easier to understand. You are essentially orbiting the kettlebell around the back of your head and bringing it back in front of you to the starting position.

Bent over row – This is another exercise you are probably familiar with if you have been working out for a little bit. The only difference is you are using this exercise with a kettlebell(s) instead of dumbbells or a barbell. Star by bending over with your back straight. Then pick up the kettlebell and raise it straight up. Bring your elbow straight up so that it's at the height of your back or higher. Controlling the movement of kettlebell is crucial to this exercise so that it's effective for you.

Chapter 8: Kettlebell Exercises

10 Kettlebell Exercises

Kettlebells has gained wide popularity as it has proven to be beneficial for cardio, strength and flexibility training. Now there are various sizes of kettlebells and techniques which an individual need to understand to achieve their goals. It is usually suggested that women should start by lifting 8-16kg weights and men should start with 16 to 32 kg. However, the number of reps and sets are depended on the level of fitness required. Thanks for the technology, you can watch how to do these move correctly! Moreover, there are various types of kettlebell exercises that are discussed in detail below:

Russian Kettlebell Swing: This exercise is recommended for beginner and targets shoulders, back, hips and legs. To achieve accurate kettlebell swing, the posture should be straight in standing position with feet a bit wider than hip-distance apart. Once the posture is set, hold the handle of the kettlebell with both hands and keep the palms facedown and arms in front of the body. Maintain a slight bend to the knee and drive the hips back and lowering the body. It is important to make sure that this is not too low. Then, in a fluid motion, keeping the glutes and core engaged, explosively drive the hips forward while swinging the kettlebell. Along with this, it is imperative to ensure that the motion should not come from the arm but from the hips, as the body returns to standing. This swing should continue for 12-15 reps while lowering the weight back down between the legs. Furthermore, since it is for beginners, the weight of the kettlebell should be appropriate to avoid any injury. Example in this video.

Kettlebell Figure-8: This exercise is suggested for intermediate level and focuses on the arms, back, and abs of an individual. In order to do it accurately, it is important to keep the back straight and chest up while keeping legs a bit wider than hip-width distance apart. The correct position will be lowering the body into a quarter-squat position. Whereas, people often misunderstood the position and keep the position as it is in a squat. Once the position is set, hold the kettlebell with the left hand, swing it around the outside of the left leg, and then back between the legs. Now do the exact exercise with the right hand and keep the motion going. In this swing, it is essential to ensure that the shift from left to right hand is done halfway through. Example in this video.

Kettlebell Goblet Squat: It is the most common type of swing, which targets legs, back, and glutes. This type of squat is for intermediate level and requires a straight position. The kettlebell is kept in front of the chest with both hands while keeping the elbows close to the body. Now start the squats by driving the heels into the ground and pushing the hips back until the thighs are parallel to the ground or just below. This should be continued for 15-20 reps. A lot of people find this easy and aim for more reps without worrying about the right posture. However, the focus should be more on the quality rather than the quantity of swing. Example in this video .

Kettlebell High Pull: This exercise focuses on the shoulders, arms, glutes, and legs. It is for intermediate level and beginners are not encouraged to try it initially. To do this properly, kettlebell should be kept on the ground between both legs and toes should be turned out 45 degrees with feet a bit wider than shoulder-width apart. Now start squatting while keeping the core engaged. The handle of the kettlebell should be controlled using one hand only. Then, using force from the hips, push through the heels to rise to standing, pulling the kettlebell in the upward position while the elbow drives up. After this, lower back down and switch arms. The aim should be for 10 to 12 for each arm. Example in this video.

Kettlebell Clean: This exercise is for advanced level and beginners are highly recommended not to try this on their first attempt. As it is of high intensity and might cause injury to people who are not trained. It focuses on legs, butt, and back. This is why people who have back injury are not encouraged to do it. Now to do the exercise accurately, it is instructed to start the swing in upward position between the feet. Shrug the shoulders, pulling the body and 'bell up to the shoulder. The 'bell should end in the "rack" position: resting on the forearm, which is tucked close to the body, the fist at your chest. Now, this should be repeated for 10-15 reps while bringing the kettlebell down to the ground. In addition to this, kettlebell clean is considered one of the most beneficial exercises as it helps to build shoulder strength and core. It provides a good conditioning effect if is continued for a long period. Example is in this video.

Single-Arm Kettlebell Split Jerk: It is important to ensure that knees can bear pressure, as the primary focus of this exercise is shoulders, chest, back, and legs. In case the position is not correct then it might hurt the back and legs. Therefore, it is for advanced level. Start by cleaning the kettlebell to the shoulder, finishing with the palm-facing front. After this, press the kettlebell overhead in bending position while jumping into a split jerk position steadily. Now return to standing position and keep kettlebell remains overhead, and then lower the weight. Repeat this exercise for 4 to 6 on each side for people who are doing for the first time. Example is in this video.

Two-Arm Kettlebell Military Press: This is the most advanced exercise of kettlebell training that is defined as a high-intensity workout as it requires two kettlebells. It helps to gain power, strength, and flexibility of the body. It involves big and small muscles. In addition, it generates power from the core outward to the object attempting to control. The focus is towards the shoulders, arms, and back of the body. Now to start the exercise, hold the kettlebells and clean them to the "rack" position. It is important to ensure that the grip of kettlebells is strong. After this, move the kettlebells in an upward position while leaning forward at the waist so the weights are positioned behind the head. Bring the kettlebells back on the shoulder and repeat this for 10 to 20 reps. In this exercise is it crucial to select the right size of kettlebell to avoid any injury in hands. Example is in this video.

Kettlebell Push-Up with Row: This advanced level exercise requires a push-up position. It targets chest, back, and arms of the body. It is very important to have the right position. Now in the push-up position, hold the kettlebell in the right arm and perform a push-up. At the top, lift the right elbow by squeezing the shoulder blades together with the weight about six inches behind the body. Once this is done properly, return to the position and repeat this for 5 to 8 reps with left and right arm. People often make mistake in making the right posture, which makes it difficult to perform the push up accurately. Example is in this video.

Kettlebell Windmill: An advanced level exercise that focuses on the Shoulders, back, abs, oblique's, and hips. To do this exercise properly, place a kettlebell in front of the lead foot, clean, and press it overhead with opposite arm. Clean the kettlebell towards shoulder by extending through the legs and hips as the kettlebell is pulled towards the shoulders. Now, rotate the wrist, so that the palm faces forward. Press it overhead by extending the elbow. Keeping the kettlebell locked out at all times, push the butt out in the direction of the locked out kettlebell. Turn feet out at a forty-five-degree angle from the arm with the locked out kettlebell. Bending at the hip to one side, sticking the butt out, slowly lean until the floor is touched with the free hand. The common mistake people make in this exercise is to maintain the posture, which is similar to triangular pose, or maintain the control of the body. Example is in this video.

Side Step Kettlebell Swing: This exercise is for intermediate and advanced level depending on the size of the kettlebell. The targets of the swing are legs, glutes, back of the body. In the initial step, hold the kettlebell with both the hands and start with the basic two-handed swing. Now bring the legs together when the bell is down between the feet, step the right foot out to the right; then, when the bell is up, bring the left foot to meet the right. Repeat this for 10 – 15 reps and then use the left foot to do the exercise. The most common mistake people often make is that they ignore the position of the legs that need to be close to each other during the exercise. Example is in this video.

Chapter 9: A Few Other Essentials

We have provided all of the essential information through this book in regards to the kettlebell. You should be very familiar with what kettlebells are and the different variations they come in. While there is no one-size fits all kettlebell or style, there are certain key qualities you should be looking for. We have discussed all of this in the previous chapters. In addition, the exercises and workout schedules will provide amazing results that you will benefit from for the rest of your life. Use your newfound knowledge and love for this amazing tool to create many health and fitness goals. I believe in you.

Before I close out the book completely, I want to tie up some loose ends. I will detail some extra essential information that was not able to be touched on in previous chapters. Also, I will reinforce some information that needs extra attention. My hope is that I cover as many aspects of the kettlebell as possible so you feel informed and can proceed in a confident manner.

I stated earlier that a good quality kettlebell can run anywhere between 50 to 300 dollars. If you are only looking to use it once in a while, then one or two kettlebells should serve you well. My hope is that you make the kettlebell part of your regular routine. Performing the various exercises we have detailed at least three or four times a week will provide you with tremendous results. If you are serious about your kettlebell training, then definitely get multiple kettlebells of varying weights. This will increase your ability to change things up on a daily basis by performing exercises at different levels. You can also build up your stamina in a major way.

In order to make the kettlebell work for you, there are some fundamental principles to follow. Pay special attention to these well before you start any exercises with them. Following these guidelines will help you put together a solid training routine. From here, you will have a strong foundation to build off of for the rest of your life.

Progressive training is crucial. Progress over time and never try to take on more than you can handle. Your body will not adjust and adapt properly and you will not feel comfortable in the workouts. Plus you risk major injury. Exercise will make you tired, sore, and even cause some pain. In the end, it should not make you feel worse. Challenge yourself for sure by pushing a little bit extra each day, but do not skip steps while you are progressing.

Pay attention to your repetitions. A common goal many people have during weight training is to aim for muscle failure. This means to work out a specific muscle to the point it can no longer handle the workload. You may have seen people at the gym doing as many repetitions as they can on the bench press or other weight equipment until they can no longer physically lift it. Doing this repeatedly puts a great amount of stress on the body which can lead to multiple health consequences down the line. Do not aim for muscle failure. Instead, make your goal about 12-15 reps using a diversity of weights and varying moves. Start with a small number of reps and then move up as tolerated. Do this with each session and you will always get a full-body workout.

I have enforced and reinforced the importance of proper form. I will mention it again because it is so important. People become so impatient with trying to learn different exercises that they don't learn proper form. Stick to this rule rigidly. I don't care how quickly you progress through the exercises. I care about how safe you are keeping yourself. Don't get lazy on your form.

Mix up your routine on a daily basis. Do not perform the same workout every single day. Keep your body guessing by routinely adding more reps, changing the sets, performing new moves, and using different weights. If you don't mix things up, your body will become stagnant and your results will plateau.

Train barefoot on a hardwood floor. This may seem odd, but there is a significant reason behind it. A load-bearing force needs a solid base to disperse. Unfortunately, most shoes have soles that are too soft or allow your feet to move around constantly in them. Exercising barefoot will make a huge difference. Of course, you may need to wear shoes at times, like if the floor is not made for being barefoot or you are using a public gym. If you are at home, consider using a thin exercise mat that still provides some firmness.

One of the great things about exercising is that it allows you to make goals and then reach them. When you start making accomplishments with your exercise routines, it helps to build your self-confidence. One way that you can keep track of your achievements is by writing them down. Journaling is a great activity that complements exercise.

TRAINING VIDEOS AND CLASSES

While I contend that you will have a blast working out with a kettlebell, it can certainly become mundane for some people without some type of external stimulation. To incorporate this, you can do things like exercise outside or listen to music. Further options include kettlebell training videos and classes, both private and public. These options also offer guidance and support, in case you may need it.

I hope that I was able to give you enough information and confidence in this book, so you won't need these options. However, if you still want to pursue this route, I certainly understand. I have been working out my whole life and I definitely recognize the importance of having a support system, like a gym buddy or trainer, to make things easier. In these instances, training videos and classes can provide great assistance. Each of these options provides some type of advantage over the other. Before you go any of these routes, please consider some of these pros and cons.

Pros of kettlebell training videos:

Training videos are in high abundance and can be found very easily. Your best bet is to order online. In addition, many online streaming options can provide great videos too.

They are very affordable. In fact, you may even be able to find some for free online. I am talking about legal options here. If you can't find them for free without breaking a law, then you can still find them for just a few bucks.

They provide the knowledge and expertise you get from a class or trainer, but allow you to perform exercises in your own home. Imagine being in your living room watching a video, and feeling like you are in a class, without actually being in a class.

You can play these videos at any time of the day, so the convenience factor is great.

If you want to learn personally from an expert, but are self-conscious around other people, then you can still receive expert level help in the privacy of your own home.

Videos can be easy to follow because they are doing the routines as they are explaining them. In fact, if the video is not showing you the routines, don't even consider them.

Cons of kettlebell training videos:

There are many poorly done videos out there that provide inept information, and showcase bad form and technique. You really have to do your research before buying and read the reviews if available. Even with videos, there are many con artists who try to take advantage of people.

While watching someone on screen performing the routines can be educational and informative, it won't provide the same experience as a real-life class or personal training session.

Pros of kettlebell classes and personal trainers:

Obviously, with both options you are being trained by a professional who can watch you closely and correct your form. Even in a class setting with multiple people, the personal attention can be quite obvious.

The workouts can be personalized and tailored to your own needs. We are all individuals and require varying levels of attention. Some people may have limitations of some sort. Working with a real-life trainer can help overcome these obstacles. This is especially true when working with a personal trainer.

If you are someone who does not want to invest in exercise equipment for the home, then being able to go to the gym and use their equipment is a plus. Usually, any good gym and/or trainer will have good equipment that works well for your needs. Again, do your research before buying a membership.

A class can provide a great amount of support. When there are other people who have similar fitness goals as you, it can become a very friendly and welcoming environment. A training class can become a place where you get to socialize a little bit too and even create some lifelong friendships. You can start encouraging one another and even learn from each other. Just make sure the socializing does not distract you from your workouts.

It's a great excuse for getting out of the house. If you are someone who loves getting out of the house, why not be productive and join a class?

Cons of kettlebell classes and personal trainers:

They can be very expensive. This is especially true of personal trainers. Many of these personalized classes can end up costing more than a gym membership. This is another reason you must do your research and make sure it's something you want to pursue. Once you start seeing the prices of various classes and personal trainers, the cost of a kettlebell won't seem too steep. There is a caveat here. Many gyms offer occasional classes like these as part of their memberships. Also, many community or recreational centers offer classes for free or a very reduced price. Consider these avenues as well.

Time becomes a factor. you will no longer have the convenience of working out at home and saving an immense amount of time. You have to dedicate time to actually go to the gym or wherever the class is being held. This requires a lot more discipline. In addition, you are at the mercy of the gym hours. If you like to get a workout done in the morning or late at night, this may not be an option if the times of the facility do not work out. Plus, you must take into account the drive time and the process of getting ready.

You will lack the privacy that you would have enjoyed being in your own home. Yes, while being around other people can be fun, privacy during a workout can be appealing. If you are someone who hates working out in front of people for no reason, this can become difficult for you. You will either have to overcome this setback or choose a different option. The freedom to work out in your home as you please also goes away.

While you may meet some exceptional people in your class, you may also have to deal with rude people too. This is something you will have very little control over.

The instructor may be a fraud, or at least someone who is not right for you. Not everyone will be your cup of tea, and this includes trainers.

Sanitary conditions are something to consider. During a class, pay attention to the cleanliness of the facility. This is a major health concern.

Once again, I hope you have the confidence and desire after reading through this book to be able to work out at home with the kettlebell. One of the most appealing things about this tool is how easily it can fit anywhere in your home. The convenience it provides is all the more reason to consider buying your own kettlebell. However, these options are still good. If you choose one of these routes, strongly consider the pros and cons of each and make your own informed decision. I am here to support you either way.

COMPLEMENTING THE KETTLEBELL

The kettlebell is great for our health and wellness. We will look and feel great after incorporating these workouts into our regular routine. However, exercise alone is not the key to complete health. We have to consider other factors. For this final section, we will discuss some supplements and nutritional information that will complement the kettlebell workouts.

Our body needs fuel and we need to make sure we are filling up with the essential nutrients we need. Doing this will get you much better results than exercise alone.

While none of our bodies are alike, if you work out hard, but then eat nothing but donuts, cheeseburgers, pizza, and other unhealthy foods, you will not benefit from the kettlebell as you should. You won't obtain the same tone or have the right amount of energy. Treat your body like a temple by exercising regularly and being careful about what you take in.

Crucial Supplements

We will begin by discussing the most important supplements to take in while performing intense kettlebell training. A combination of these will provide for adequate energy, muscle building and rebuilding, recovery processes, as well as numerous other necessary functions. High level workouts can be traumatic for the body so we need to make sure we supply it with all of the necessities it needs for continued support. The following are essential supplements to complement our kettlebell workouts.

Protein Powder:

Whey protein powder is the most popular option and also a very good one. This is often associated with body-builders and very high-level athletes, so many people do not think of it as essential because those are not their workout goals. Whey protein powder adds more value than just becoming ripped and huge.

Protein is the building block of your body. It can help to rebuild muscles, which is sorely needed after major workouts with all of the muscle breakdown. This supplement also increases energy to help you live and function. This will help you immensely with your activities of daily living.

Whey protein also strengthens your immune system, so many minor and major illnesses may start avoiding you completely. I am not a doctor, so I am not making any promises here. However, protein is essential for improving health function. You will improve your muscle performance, increase strength, detoxify your body, and recover much more quickly. Many people do not realize the amount of waste that builds up in the body with muscle breakdown. If you work out intensely with the kettlebell, this will happen to you for sure. Detoxifying the body will help here in a major way.

All of these benefits are essential and will help you maximize your kettlebell workouts. If you have not been incorporating protein supplements into your diet, then you need to rethink things completely. Start including it now before you get into any heavy duty kettlebell workouts. Any top-level athlete takes in a lot of protein because of how important the supplement is

L-Carnitine:

This can also simply be called carnitine and is an essential nutrient which will aid in the burning of fat. This will help give fuel to your body functions and workouts. Kettlebell training already burns massive amounts of calories and builds muscle mass all by itself. Getting this extra kick from carnitine to burn excess fat will make you even more toned and shredded.

Carnitine helps drive fat into the cells. From here, it goes into the mitochondria, which is the powerhouse of the cell, and gets burned to produce more energy. This means less visceral and subcutaneous fat.

Low carnitine levels have been associated with major muscle dysfunctions. Many more studies are being done to assess carnitine's effectiveness in elevating muscle performance. Carnitine also boosts recovery and can lower your risk of heart disease. This is another supplement you definitely don't want to dismiss, especially when you start performing kettlebell workouts.

Creatine:

Creatine is definitely critical when starting kettlebell workouts. This supplement prevents premature fatigue of the fast-twitch fibers in the muscles. This means you will greatly strengthen your muscle contractions and enhance your endurance.

You will be able to perform many more reps during your kettlebell workouts. Muscle strength and tone will increase tremendously from here.

Creatine also increases anaerobic capacity, so you won't lose your breath so quickly. This nutrient also enhances the recovery process, increases cognitive function, and elevates bone recovery levels. Consider the great value all of this will bring to complement your kettlebell training.

Branched Chain Amino Acids (BCAA):

BCAAs consist of three amino acids called leucine, isoleucine, and valine. These amino acid chains help build muscles, reduce soreness after workouts, decrease the period of recovery needed, and improve workout performance. Once again, all essential benefits when starting up kettlebell training.

BCAAs increase the rate of protein synthesis by stimulating some key enzymes and help build muscles while reducing the rate of muscle loss. The anabolic effects also help increase muscle strength and size. Imagine how much more muscle mass you can achieve by adding this supplement to your diet.

BCAAs also improve exercise performance by reducing your chances of getting fatigued prematurely. They help burn excess fat instead of glycogen stores reserved to fuel muscle cells.

Caffeine:

Caffeine is the final supplement for discussion today. I don't mean just drinking large amounts of coffee or soda here. Of course, a cup or two of some good coffee can be great. However, small amounts of caffeine can be quite beneficial. This supplement will boost metabolism and also have thermogenic effects on the body, which will melt more body fat. Thermogenesis is the process of taking in the calories you eat and converting them to heat energy. It is not completely understood how caffeine promotes thermogenesis, however, the advantages it gives for burning calories and fat. Go ahead and drink that cup of coffee in the morning without feeling guilty. Just watch out for the sweetener and creamer.

Many of these supplements can be found at your local vitamin store. Follow the instructions on how to take them and begin boosting your kettlebell training. I always recommend seeking out the advice of a medical professional before starting supplements. Even though they are over-the-counter, they can still have negative effects under certain circumstances. This is especially true if you have underlying health conditions or take other medications. When you are ready, start taking these amazing supplements.

NUTRITION TIPS AND GUIDANCE

The last topic I want to discuss here today is nutrition. There is a major myth out there that if you exercise hard enough, you can eat anything and everything you want. This mindset is wrong and also dangerous. Even if you are diligent with your workouts, a poor diet can still have detrimental effects on your health. This can include heart disease, stroke, diabetes and even certain types of cancer. Also, a poor diet will reduce your energy level, mess with your digestion, and negatively affect your sleep. If you get several hours of sleep every night but still feel exhausted all day, you may need to alter what food you intake. You cannot ignore this fact.

Eating properly with the correct nutrients will also enhance the results from a good workout. If you are training constantly but getting no results, your diet is what might be holding you back. We discussed protein powder in the previous section. You can also start eating more protein-rich foods like lean meat, poultry, eggs, or plant-based proteins like soy or tofu. Eat that extra protein and you will start bulking up and building lean muscle in no time.

Start eliminating carbs from your diet. This is especially true of refined sugars, white rice, white bread and white pasta. Your body will naturally use carbs for energy. When you reduce the number of carbs in your diet, you will have less in the body. This means your body will start utilizing fat for energy so you will start burning high levels of it.

Make sure you are counting your calories every day and keep a record of this somewhere. You will need either a calorie surplus or deficit depending on fitness goals. Remember, with kettlebell workouts, you will be torching those calories big time, so you may need to intake more.

Simply cutting out many of the garbage foods we eat every day can make a huge difference. You don't have to make drastic changes right away, but making small alterations here and there will create amazing results for you. Start drinking more water. In fact, replace many of the sugary drinks with pure water and your body will thank you. also, trade those salty and sugary snacks for things like raw almonds, or vegetables. Finally, don't eat a big meal right before going to bed. Eat your last major meal at least two hours before going to bed and then you can just eat a small snack like Greek yogurt later on. Having a small healthy snack right before bed will increase your metabolism while you sleep, which can also result in fat loss. These are just a few suggestions to start making significant changes in your life.

Unfortunately, due to busy schedules and the convenience that comes with unhealthy foods, people simply ignore the importance of a proper diet. Going through the drive-thru at the local fast food joint is more appealing than going home and cooking a fresh meal after a long day. It will take some effort, but the results will be worth it.

Many people stick to the schedule of breakfast, lunch and dinner and eat heavily during each meal. A better option is to break down the meals throughout the day. This means you can have a moderate-sized breakfast, lunch, and dinner with a light healthy snack in between. This will keep your metabolism going throughout the day and allow you to function better by keeping up your energy levels.

Consider some of the diet plans that exist around the country. The word diet has a negative connotation to it. However, there are several that have stood the test of time. Take the Mediterranean diet as an example. This plan originates from the region surrounding the Mediterranean Sea in Europe and has been around for centuries. Like the kettlebell, it began getting popular around the world over the last several decades when people began understanding the major health benefits it possessed. The diet also boasts bold and flavorful ingredients. You will never have to sacrifice taste for health. The food groups and ingredients used in this meal plan will provide all of the essential nutrients you need without the excess sugar, fat, and cholesterol. Research the Mediterranean diet and consider including it in your own life.

Remember, what you fuel your body with is important. The food we eat and the nutrients we take in are what allow us to keep functioning. You would not want to fill your car gas tank with inferior gasoline, if there is such a thing. Do not fill yourself up with bad fuel either. Treat your body like a temple and take care of it in every aspect. You only get one.

Chapter 10: Making Your Metabolism Work For You

Your weight loss goals are largely dependent on your metabolic rate. When working out to lose weight, you should not focus on the amount of calories you lose per workout. Instead, focus on increasing your metabolic rate every day. By doing this, you will maximize the effect of your workout by burning calories all throughout the day.

People who live a sedentary lifestyle have a difficult time losing weight because they spend most of their time in a rested state. When we rest, our body tries to conserve energy by making our metabolism slower. It is at its slowest when we are asleep.

Increasing your metabolism

Every time you work out, your body not only spends energy to do your reps and laps but it also spends it to repair your body afterwards. The repair and maintenance process that our body enters after a workout increases our metabolic rate. Your metabolism is the overall chemical processes that your body performs for its maintenance. The amount of chemical reactions that happen in your body is momentarily increased after your workouts to repair the body and to make it stronger the next time around. This increased metabolic rate means that your body is spending energy even though we are no longer working out.

For people who want to grow bigger muscles, it is essential to rest immediately after working out. The rest period allows our body to focus its attention on repair and maintenance. After it is done with what it needs to do, the body gradually returns to a normal metabolic rate.

If you want to lose weight, you must prolong the periods of high metabolic rate. This period shortens if you rest or sleep after your workouts. If you remain awake and active after a high-intensity workout however, you can prolong this period.

To maximize the effects of your workout routines, you should schedule your workouts in the morning before you go to the office. The high intensity workouts suggested in this book will speed up your metabolism early in the morning. This increased metabolic rate will continue even as you go to work. Your heart rate will be faster than usual. You will be spending more energy in your office time until your body has done all the repairs and maintenance that it needs to do.

Some people who aren't used to working out in the morning become easily winded out when they start this habit. Over time however, you will be used to the feeling and you will be able to work through it.

Chapter 11: Cooling Down

Even if they warm-up properly, many people tend to neglect cooling down after a workout. After all, the warm-up was the important one of the two, so you can just let your muscles cool down at their own pace, right? Not really, warming up and cooling down properly are equally important. It is crucial that you don't skip your cool down for any reason. Whether you just don't feel like it or perhaps you're strapped for time, it doesn't matter what the reason is, your body needs that cool down session.

Cooling down after a hard workout benefits you in a variety of ways.

PREVENT BLOOD POOLING

When you are performing a hard workout, your blood vessels dilate and your heart rate accelerates. This causes a higher volume of blood to be pumped around your body. When blood is being pumped to your extremities, gravity is there to help. When the blood is pumped back up to your heart, gravity works against the flow. This is where the movement of your body and muscles come in to help. The squeeze and release pressure created by your muscles moving helps to keep the blood pumping back up to your heart and lungs to be re-oxygenated.

When you suddenly stop and skip your cool down after a workout, so does that squeeze and release action, slowing the flow of blood back up to your heart, lungs, and even your brain. Blood begins to pool in your lower extremities and takes time to be pumped back. This not only deprives your body of a sufficient amount of oxygenated blood flowing to all areas, it creates a further problem for your body.

Your arteries and veins contain valves that work in only one direction so that blood cannot flow backward, it can only keep flowing in the direction it is meant to flow in. When you suddenly stop exercising, the pressure that kept the blood flowing also stops, and there isn't enough pressure to keep the blood flowing. Pooling blood becomes trapped between the valves in your blood vessels.

Your heart rate slows and doesn't pump as hard and fast, your muscles aren't applying pressure to help the blood move along, and your blood vessels take time to increase pressure by contracting again to accommodate a lower volume of blood flow. All of this put together can lead to dizziness, feeling light-headed, and even fainting.

DELAYED ONSET MUSCLE SORENESS (DOMS)

When you exercise and push your muscles and body, the result is micro-tears in the muscle fibers. This is completely normal and something that you actually want to have happen. In order for the muscle to rebuild itself stronger than before, it needs to be broken down first. Within 24 to 48 hours after developing these micro-tears in the muscle tissue, you will experience that all too familiar muscle soreness. This is known as delayed onset muscle soreness (DOMS).

Muscle soreness is a given, even desirable, but there comes a point at which it is no longer a slight discomfort. Muscle soreness may become intolerable and prevent you from keeping up with your workout schedule or even performing some daily tasks. This level of DOMS is undesirable and can be lessened or avoided altogether with a proper cool down after your workout.

Cooling down properly helps to keep your blood flowing after your workout. This works to lessen or prevent DOMS by keeping a sufficient supply of oxygen and nutrient-rich blood flowing to your muscles.

DOMS is a good sign that your workout is doing the job of building stronger muscle and advancing your progress. However, more muscle soreness doesn't necessarily translate to more muscle being rebuilt. If DOMS lingers for more than two or three days, it could indicate that you are overtraining, are suffering from an illness, or that you are vulnerable to injury. Listening to your body is key to keeping you safe, injury-free, and on track with your workout routine.

RELIEVING STRESS

Many people find exercise to be a form of decompressing and lightening their stress load. Exercising helps fight stress by releasing serotonin and dopamine, your body's natural hormones that make you feel good. You receive the maximum benefit of that feel-good effect when you cool down adequately after a workout instead of coming to a grinding halt immediately after. Your cool down is also a great space of time to breathe and mentally prepare yourself for heading back to life with a fresh, focused mind.

PREVENT INJURIES

Everybody says that warming up is the best way to prevent injuries during your workout. Warm, pliable muscles are less prone to injury than cold, stiff muscles. Cooling down properly is equally as important to aid in injury prevention. Stretching warm muscles after a workout will help you achieve greater flexibility. Over time, with consistent cool down stretching, the muscles will naturally lengthen which provides you with a wider range of motion.

Greater flexibility and a wider range of motion helps prevent injuries in two ways. The first is that you are less likely to become injured during your workout or while performing normal daily activities. The second is that it helps combat common aches and pains such as back pain. Short or inflexible hamstrings and hip flexors are often the culprits that cause backache. By cooling down and working on these muscles, you can effectively lessen back pain.

BETTER RECOVERY

Lactic acid builds up in your body during a hard workout. It also takes time to make its way out of your system again after a workout. By cooling down properly, you help speed up the process of removing that lactic acid buildup.

THE COOL DOWN

JOGGING AND WALKING

Bring your body back down to earth after a good workout by taking a very light jog or brisk walk for approximately three to five minutes. This will help keep your body moving at a slower pace while your heart rate comes down, your breathing slows down, and your body begins its natural cooling down process.

STRETCHING

Stretching is a great way to cool down, your muscles are warmed up and in prime condition to make full use of some good stretches.

Cross Chest Arm Swing

This cool down exercise can be performed while you are taking a brisk walk to cool down. Alternatively, you can keep moving by stepping side to side for the duration of this exercise.

Swing your arms forward to cross your chest and the front of your body.

Going in the opposite direction to complete the swing motion, swing your arms as far back behind you as possible without straining or discomfort.

Maintain a regular rhythm but don't be overzealous, keep the swing at a medium pace.

Side Bench Stretch

Stand in a relaxed, neutral position with your arms at your sides and feet a little wider than shoulder-width apart.

Shift your weight over onto your right hip, pushing that hip out slightly.

Lean your torso over to the left and extend your right arm to the left, over your head.

Change sides and repeat the stretch.

Cross Body Shoulder Stretch

Stand in a relaxed, neutral position with your arms at your sides and feet shoulder-width apart.

Reach your right arm across the front of your chest at about or just below shoulder height. Make sure that your arm and elbow are straight.

Use your left hand to hold your right arm at the elbow, pulling the arm towards your chest until you can feel the stretch in your right shoulder. Don't pull too hard, gently increase the pressure until you feel the stretch.

Swap sides and repeat the stretch on the left side.

Overhead Triceps Stretch

Stand in a relaxed, neutral position with your arms at your sides and feet shoulder-width apart.

Reach your right arm over your right shoulder, bending at the elbow to touch the top of your shoulder.

Using your left arm, reach over your head to hold your right elbow.

Apply gentle pressure to pull your right elbow back until you feel the stretch down your triceps.

Switch sides and repeat the stretch.

Wide Toe Touch

Stand in a relaxed, neutral position with your arms at your sides and feet about twice shoulder-width apart.

Bend forward from your hips and bend over as far forward as possible. If you can touch your toes or grab the backs of your ankles, that's great. If you can't, bend forward as far as you can until you can feel the stretch in your hamstrings.

Using your core muscles, straighten up back to a standing position.

As a variation to this stretch, you can cross your arm over to touch your left foot toes and then cross your left arm to touch your foot right toes. If you choose to do this variation, hold the stretch to each side for half the total recommended stretch time.

Gluteal Stretch

This stretch can be tricky if you don't have great balance. If you have trouble wobbling or falling over, perform this stretch near a wall, chair, or other support that you can hold on to for balance.

Stand in a relaxed, neutral position with your arms at your sides and feet shoulder-width apart.

Raise your left leg and cross your left ankle just above your right knee.

Squat down slightly by bending your right knee and slowly moving into a semi-squat position.

Lean your torso slightly forward and extend your arms in front of you to help with balance. Don't lean too far forward.

Keep lowering yourself into the squat position until you feel the stretch in your gluteal muscles.

Change sides and repeat the stretch.

Quad Stretch

Stand in a relaxed, neutral position with your arms at your sides and feet shoulder-width apart.

Shift your weight onto your right leg.

Bend your left knee and bring your left foot to your bottom. Keep your left thigh in line with your right thigh and keep them close together. Don't let your left thigh come forward or drift outwards.

Reach around with your left hand to grab your left ankle, gently applying pressure by pulling your ankle further towards your bottom until you can feel the stretch in your quadriceps.

Swap sides and repeat the stretch on the right side.

Inner Thigh Stretch

Stand in a relaxed, neutral position with your arms at your sides and feet twice shoulder-width apart.

Move your weight onto your right leg and push your right hip outwards towards the right. This should cause your left leg to lengthen and straighten.

Bend your right knee and drop your left hip towards the floor until you feel the stretch in your left inner thigh. Keep your left leg straight to the side.

Switch sides and repeat the stretch on the left side.

Hip Flexor Stretch

Stand in a relaxed, neutral position with your arms at your sides and feet shoulder-width apart.

Move into a regular lunge position but keep your back leg straight instead of bending the knee.

Keep your back straight and chest up.

Lean forward into the lunge until you feel the stretch across your hip.

Change sides and repeat the stretch on the other side.

Wall Stretch

Stand in front of a wall in a relaxed, neutral position with your arms at your sides and feet shoulder-width apart.

Raise both arms and place your hands against the wall shoulder-width apart and a little above head height.

Step backward with one leg, stretching out your arms, shoulders, and chest.

Keeping the back leg straight, lean your hips downward into the stretch to feel it in your calves and hamstrings.

Step forward with your back leg, change sides, and step back with the other leg to repeat the stretch on the other side.

HOW LONG SHOULD YOU COOL DOWN?

Your cool down session should last between two and 15 minutes and consist of stretches that target the main muscle groups used in your workout. If you feel that you have inflexible or tight muscles, spend some extra time focusing on the stretches that work those problem areas to increase flexibility and range of motion.

COOL DOWN ROUTINE

Jog/walk	3 – 5 minutes
Cross Chest Arm Swing	30 seconds

Side Bench Stretch	30 seconds per side
Cross Body Shoulder Stretch	30 seconds per side
Overhead Triceps Stretch	30 seconds per side
Wide Toe Touch	30 seconds
Gluteal Stretch	30 seconds per side
Quad Stretch	30 seconds per side
Inner Thigh Stretch	30 seconds per side
Hip Flexor Stretch	30 seconds per side
Wall Stretch	30 seconds per side

Chapter 12: Training Hacks

While formal training methods yield the biggest results, there are certain lifestyle changes that can increase your fitness and lead to percentage increases in performance. The following chapter outlines of my favorite "hacks" that you can easily add in to your routines and life.

Grease the groove

Greasing the groove is a technique made famous by Pavel Tsatsouline. At its most basic level, greasing the groove involves doing bodyweight or weighted movements throughout the day instead of all at once.

How this works practically is doing something like mounting a pull-up bar in your bedroom doorway and repping 5 pull-ups every time you walk by. Or, maybe you do 10 push-ups every time there is a commercial break during a sports game. The idea is that you spread movements throughout the day. 10 push-ups, 10 kettlebell deadlifts and 20 air squats every hour for 8 hours in a day doesn't seem like much but it adds up in time!

One thing that I do leave a loaded barbell in my garage. Every time I get into my car I'll pull 3-5 deadlifts, do 5 pull-ups and a few walking lunges for good measure.

Gripper

Using a hand strength gripper is an easy way to create hand strength while you are at your desk or in your car. Kettlebell training requires a sturdy grip and this is an easy way to train it. While we mostly take a functional, whole body approach to this through hanging, deadlifting, and farmer carries, as three examples, using a gripper is another simple practice to add to your training.

Hang

Hanging from a bar is an excellent way to build hand and forearm strength and offers a slightly different effect than the pulling motion in a pull-up. Like with greasing the groove, consider taking a 30 second hang break every so often throughout the day - it will create some insane results in your training.

Farmer carry variations

Farmer carries are an excellent way to build power and grip endurance. There are some ways to bring it to the next level.

A simple thing to do is to use kettlebell or dumbbells of different weights in each hand, so a 50 lb. in your right hand and a 60 lb. in your left. This will force you to compensate for the different weights by engaging your core so you will activate more musculature. Another reason to do different weights - farmer carries in races will often be with odd objects that may be off by 5 or so pounds. Train like you race.

Apart from the different weights, experiment with using other grip methods. Attach vertical or horizontal pipes, balls or use thicker grips. Switch between dumbbells and kettlebells.

One of my favorite things to do is to wrap a band through 2 or 3 light weight kettlebell handles and carry by the band. This is an amazing way to fire up your grip and arms.

50 KB swing finisher

Finishing a workout with 50 kettlebell swings is an easy calorie and grip burner. It ill spike your heart rate, work your hands and forearms and activate your posterior chain and core, which can lead to quick gains in strength and durability.

Weighted Vest

Wearing a **weighted vest** while working out is a way to create more tension and burn while in a workout. By weighing down your basic movements, you can grow strength in your core and legs especially. A long ruck in a weighted vest is one of the simplest ways to gain power endurance and stamina.

I like to think of it like weighting a baseball bat before stepping to the plate. When you do this, it makes the lighter bat swing faster - working out with a weighted vest can be a similar effect.

Skill practice

We learn skills by practice. If we want to get better at something we need repetition - the same goes with our training. One way that I have been able to increase my work capacity and skill is by devoting 5 minutes in each training session to a sport-specific skill. I don't go into it with any expectations, just the mentality of "getting quality reps" to the best of my ability. This is how I learned to do climb rope, do double unders, muscle ups, paralette handstands and handstand walk. If you want to focus on a few things, focus on rope climbs and muscle-ups, then from there take a few gymnastics movements to practice. This will have a significant impact on your agility and speed.

Conclusion

Consistency, consistency, consistency - literally nothing else in this book matters if you don't stick with it. It's similar to the compound effect in that a few small changes repeated constantly can set off a whole chain reaction of benefits. Let me lay out a simple example of this effect. When you get up in the morning and replace your orange juice and jam on toast with two eggs and half an avocado you now have stable blood sugar, which helps you say no to that piece of birthday cake being offered at morning tea. As a result of this you are more likely to have the will power to select a healthy lunch since you are not keeling over with hunger. This little routine repeats itself a few times and soon it's a habit, with the incremental changes adding up to a huge amount over a year. Weight is generally put on over a prolonged period, so I always find it frustrating that people expect to find a silver bullet to get rid of years of excess in a few weeks. Be in it for the long game.

Which is the best exercise you can do? The one you enjoy, because you'll stick to it. I hate distance running yet love playing rugby, where in a game I can run 10km without even noticing I've done it. If you can find a sport that lights your fire, then power to you. This book outlines many effective compound exercises that if you enjoy and stick to, you will be on the path to a fitter, healthier you. I'm not saying they will be enjoyable as in easy, quite the contrary, but ultimately rewarding. Remember you only get one body so treasure it; you have to live in it every single day.

Give all the exercises in this book a try and find what doesn't work for you, what does and then keep at it. A tip I have always used is to have a piece of paper in a regularly visible place with the saying:

"What have I done today to make a difference for tomorrow?"

Thanks for reading and good luck.

Thank you again for downloading this book!

www.ingramcontent.com/pod-product-compliance
Lightning Source LLC
LaVergne TN
LVHW012000070526
838202LV00054B/4975